D0122956

IN THE SHADOW OF
LADY LIBERTY

Immigrant Stories from Ellis Island

by Danny Kravitz

Consultant:
Cindy R. Lobel, PhD
Associate Professor of History
Lehman College
Bronx, New York

CAPSTONE PRESS
a capstone imprint

Connect Books are published by Capstone Press,
1710 Roe Crest Drive, North Mankato, Minnesota 56003
www.capstonepub.com

Library of Congress Cataloging-in-Publication Data
Kravitz, Danny, 1970–
In the shadow of Lady Liberty : immigrant stories from Ellis Island / by
Danny Kravitz.
pages cm.—(Connect. U.S. immigration in the 1900s)
Summary: "Explores immigrants' experiences at Ellis Island through the
use of primary sources"—Provided by publisher.
Includes bibliographical references and index.
ISBN 978-1-4914-4127-5 (library binding)
ISBN 978-1-4914-4173-2 (paperback)
ISBN 978-1-4914-4179-4 (ebook PDF)
ISBN 978-1-4914-7890-5 (reflowable epub)
1. Ellis Island Immigration Station (N.Y. and N.J.)—History—Juvenile
literature. 2. United States—Emigration and immigration—History—Juvenile
literature. I. Title.
JV6484.K73 2016
3050.9'06912092273—dc23   2015008505

Editorial Credits
Jen Besel and Aaron Sautter, editors; Sarah Bennet, designer; Wanda Winch,
media researcher; Laura Manthe, production specialist

Photo Credits
By Courtesy of the Bob Hope Memorial Library, Ellis Island, 10-11, 26-27; Corbis:
Bettmann, 38, 41, 43, Underwood & Underwood, 7; Dreamstime: Rcavalleri, 4-5;
Getty Images/Alfred Eisenstaedt, 30, Edwin Levick, cover, Print Collecter, 14-15;
Granger, NYC, 11 (top), 12-13, 19, 20, 33, 37; Library of Congress: Prints and
Photographs Division, 8, 9, 17, 25, 29, 34; Shutterstock: ilolab, (colored textured
paper designs), LiliGraphie, (vintage wallpaper, photo tabs), nikoniano (grunge stripe
design), Sean Pavone, 44 (all); Thinkstock, 22-23

Printed in the United States of America in Stevens Point, Wisconsin.
042015   008824WZF15

TABLE OF CONTENTS

CHAPTER ONE

THE ISLAND OF VOICES

Just off the New Jersey shore, a bridge juts out into New York Harbor. That bridge leads to a small piece of land covered with empty buildings called Ellis Island. The buildings are made mostly of red and white bricks with red-shingled roofs. Trees and lawns of green grass surround them. An American flag flies high atop a flagpole waving in the wind.

The main building on this quiet island is now called the Ellis Island Museum. Its Great Hall stuns guests with large arched windows, shiny wood floors, and ceilings nearly 60 feet (18 meters) high. The building is quiet now. But the hall was once filled with millions of voices, speaking many languages.

More than 100 years ago, Ellis Island was a busy immigration station. Every day it was filled with thousands of immigrants waiting to enter the United States. These people had all left their homes and traveled thousands of miles by ship. They all had a different story but had one thing in common—they all came to America in search of better lives.

COMING TO AMERICA

A great wave of immigration flooded America's shores beginning in the 1880s and lasted roughly 40 years. Most of the travelers were from eastern and southern Europe. These immigrants were escaping poverty, religious **persecution**, and lack of job opportunity. "When someone returns from America to tell us that the wages are superior and that there are fewer discomforts, many of the men cannot resist the temptation to go and find out for ourselves," said Adolfo Russi who came to America in 1908.

Because of growing immigration, the U.S. government decided it needed a place to organize incoming immigrants. Most immigrants entered the country in New York. So a nearby island—Ellis Island—was chosen as the location of the new immigration station. When the station opened in 1892, hopeful immigrants went through an inspection process there. If all went well, they walked out the back doors of Ellis Island to start their new lives.

Albert Mardirossian, an immigrant from Armenia, arrived at Ellis Island in 1921. "You got thousands of people marching in, a little bit excited, a little bit scared. Just imagine, you're 14 and a half years old … and you don't know what's going to happen."

persecution—cruel or unfair treatment, often because of race or religious beliefs

"Just imagine, you're 14 and a half years old ...
and you don't know what's going to happen."

Chapter Two

BUILDING ELLIS ISLAND

Landing for Emigrants

Emigrants Dining Hall

Main Building, Ellis Island.

Surgeon's Residence.

Detention Room.

The government constructed and remodeled many buildings before opening Ellis Island. These included new dock landings for boats (upper left), an immigrant dining hall (upper right), a two-story main building (center), homes for doctors (lower left), detention rooms (lower right), and several others.

Before the 1890s, each state handled the immigrants who arrived at its borders. The Secretary of the Treasury, William Windom, during a meeting on immigration in 1890, said, "I felt it was my duty to have another investigation made … [immigration] could better be done by the Federal Government." Windom argued that a

William Windom

federally owned system would protect citizens from unhealthy or criminal immigrants. It would also protect immigrants from being mistreated. As Windom explained, "I preferred an island … where we could exclude those people whom we did not think [proper] to first come in contact with the immigrants landing on our shores."

The federal government already owned Ellis Island. But there was a problem. The island wasn't much more than a few acres of mud and sand. The government put $150,000 toward expanding the island and building the station. Workers dug wells for fresh water and built docks for arriving boats. They also constructed a small hospital, dormitories, kitchens, and an electric plant. A two-story main building was also constructed. "… over 4,000,000 feet of lumber have been used in its construction," stated an article in the *New-York Daily Tribune*.

◖◗ FACT ◖◗

Ellis Island was used as a military base during the War of 1812 (1812–1815). Many dangerous weapons were still there in the 1890s. The government had to clean up the weapons before building the immigration station.

A GRAND OPENING

When Ellis Island opened on January 1, 1892, it was a city unto itself. As many as 800 people had been hired to work and live on the island, including doctors, nurses, inspectors, and **interpreters**. Seven hundred immigrants passed through Ellis Island on the first day, and nearly 450,000 followed that year. "My first impression when I got there … you're in a dream," said Felice Taldone, an immigrant from Italy. "It's like in heaven. You don't know what it is. You're so happy there in America."

When Ellis Island opened, no one could have known that more than 12 million immigrants would come through its halls. Nor could they have known that disaster was about to strike.

About 1.5 million immigrants passed through Ellis Island's original central building from 1892 to 1897.

AMERICA WELCOMES ANNIE

The first immigrant to officially pass through Ellis Island was a 15-year-old Irish girl named Annie Moore. Moore journeyed from County Cork, Ireland, with her two younger brothers, Anthony and Philip. They joined their parents who were already living in New York City.

Immigrants often wore all their clothing when they traveled. They wanted to save luggage space for their family heirlooms, photographs, and other treasured keepsakes.

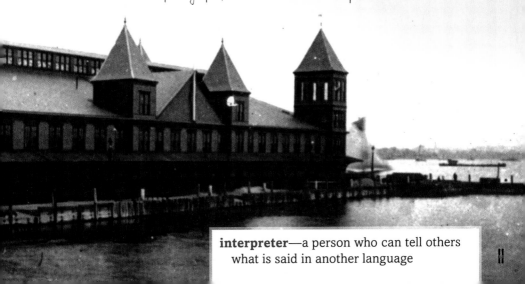

interpreter—a person who can tell others what is said in another language

FIRE!

On the night of June 14, 1897, a fire broke out on the island. Smoke appeared in the main building just after midnight. By 1:00 a.m. all the buildings were ablaze. Flames rose 100 feet (30 meters) into the night sky. Captain W. J. Burke, who was in charge of the night watch, hurried to warn people. "I rushed as quickly as possible and rang the alarm in all the rooms," he said.

◖ FACT ◗

While Ellis Island's main building was being rebuilt, immigrants were processed at the Barge Office in Battery Park in New York City.

Workers helped the nearly 200 immigrants escape the deadly heat and smoke. At least 100 tugboats arrived to rescue people from the burning island. By morning the immigration station was nothing more than a smoldering pile of rubble. No one died, but all of the records stored there were destroyed.

Since immigration wasn't slowing down, the U.S. Congress went into repair mode. It approved $600,000 to rebuild the station with fireproof buildings. Two years later, Ellis Island was reopened for immigration. It was just in time. Huge numbers of immigrants were making their way to America. On April 17, 1907, a record 11,747 immigrants passed through Ellis Island in one day. And more than 1 million came that year.

Ellis Island's new central building opened for business on December 17, 1900.

Chapter Three

GETTING TO ELLIS ISLAND

Immigrants who decided to come to America had long, difficult journeys ahead of them. They left their homes with trunks and bags filled with their belongings. Some immigrants traveled with their families. But many others had to leave their friends and families behind. "I can remember only the hustle and the bustle of those last weeks in Pinsk, the farewells from the family, the embraces and the tears," said Golda Meir, a Russian immigrant who came in 1906. "Going to America then was almost like going to the moon."

"The day I left home, my mother came with me to the railway station. When we said goodbye, she said it was like seeing me go into a casket. I never saw her again," said Julia Goniprow, a Lithuanian immigrant in 1899.

BOARDING THE SHIPS

Immigrants traveled from their homes to the nearest port. There they boarded steamships headed toward America. But before they were allowed on board, immigrants went through a short inspection process. Officials first interviewed them to collect information, including people's names, ages, and hometowns. Officials also asked if the immigrants knew anyone in America, whether they could read, and how much money they had. All this information was then written down on official forms, which became part of a ship's **manifest**.

Before boarding the ships, doctors also checked immigrants to make sure they were healthy enough to travel. Some passengers even received **vaccinations**. Then it was finally time to go.

"For me it was the unknown and it was an adventure … I probably wasn't as scared as my parents must have been. For them it was a very big move to go to a new country," said Marcia Press, a Polish immigrant. "I remember I had a back pack and I had to leave it because there was no room to put it anywhere."

manifest—a list of passengers on a ship
vaccination—a shot of medicine that protects from a disease

Immigrants were given vaccinations and checked for skin diseases before they could board a ship.

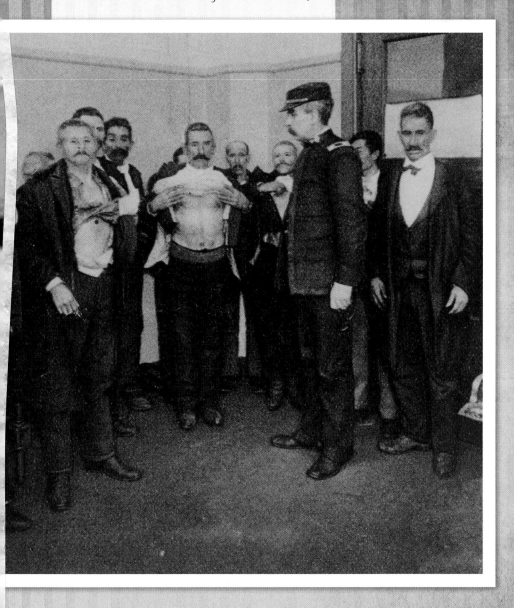

"For me it was the unknown and it was an adventure ... I probably wasn't as scared as my parents must have been. For them it was a very big move to go to a new country."

CROSSING THE ATLANTIC

Crossing the Atlantic Ocean on a steamship took between one and two weeks. Wealthy passengers traveled in comfort in first and second class. These passengers did not have to go through Ellis Island when they arrived in America.

But the poorest immigrants traveled in third class, or steerage. This area far below deck was dark and crowded. Third-class passenger Manny Steen described his experience in 1925. " … It was four in a cabin … with a tiny wash basin. Toilet was down the hall, a shower, and they served three meals a day. … There were no **amenities**, none. But you could hear the second and first class passengers having a great time up there. But we didn't care …"

The steerage section in most ships was cramped, dark, and usually smelled awful. Immigrants sometimes ate meals together in small spaces. But the food was often of poor quality. Many people became very sick during their journey to the United States.

amenities—items other than the very basic necessities

Crossing the ocean could be frightening, especially when storms hit on the high seas. William Greiner traveled to America from Italy. "It's hard for people to understand today what it was like to be on a boat then in a storm like that. … The great waves would smash, the noise tremendous, and I thought we would flounder at any moment."

But the journey could also be fun. Marcia Press remembered, "Me and another young girl went up on the deck one day and started pretending to speak English, even though we didn't know it … so we made up gibberish words and hoped the adults would think we were speaking it. Because they didn't speak English either!"

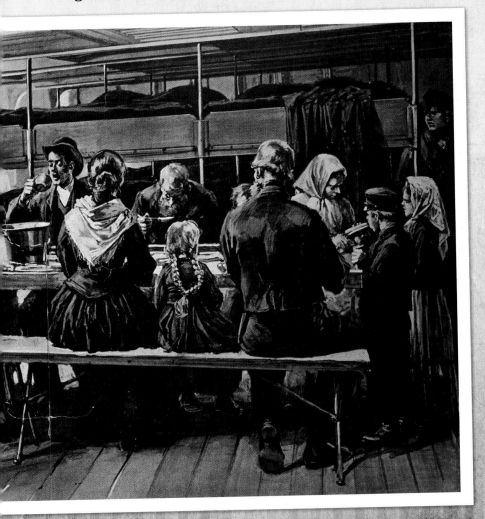

SEEING THE STATUE OF LIBERTY

For many people the hardships of the ship couldn't compare to the hardships they endured in their homelands. "That hope to be in America was so great and so sunny that it colored all the pain we had during our trip," said Gertrude Yellin, a Russian immigrant who arrived at Ellis Island in 1922.

And then they saw her. Just before landing at Ellis Island, passengers were welcomed by the sight of the Statue of Liberty. Marcia Press remembered, "Everyone cheered when we saw it. 'We were here,' we thought. 'We have finally arrived.'"

"My father and I we dressed immediately and we ran out to the deck," said Lawrence Meinwald, who arrived from Poland as a 6-year-old boy. "There were people of all [religious] denominations, some on their knees," praying as they passed the statue. "It was a great sight. … everybody was anxious, and everybody was happy, and everybody was sad."

"Everyone cheered when we saw it. 'We were here,' we thought. 'We have finally arrived.'"

For most immigrants, lady liberty was a symbol of what America offered them—hope, freedom, and the chance at a new life.

Chapter Four

INSIDE ELLIS ISLAND

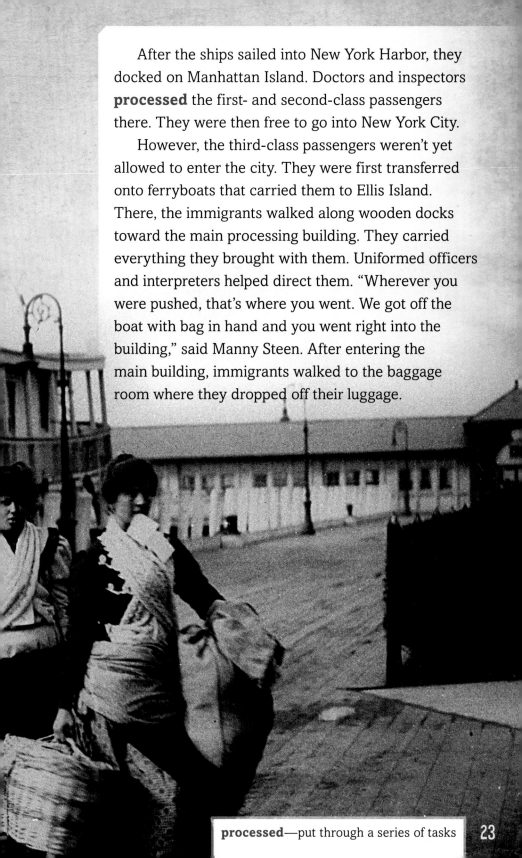

After the ships sailed into New York Harbor, they docked on Manhattan Island. Doctors and inspectors **processed** the first- and second-class passengers there. They were then free to go into New York City.

However, the third-class passengers weren't yet allowed to enter the city. They were first transferred onto ferryboats that carried them to Ellis Island. There, the immigrants walked along wooden docks toward the main processing building. They carried everything they brought with them. Uniformed officers and interpreters helped direct them. "Wherever you were pushed, that's where you went. We got off the boat with bag in hand and you went right into the building," said Manny Steen. After entering the main building, immigrants walked to the baggage room where they dropped off their luggage.

processed—put through a series of tasks

HEALTH INSPECTIONS

Immigrants walked up winding stairs that led to the Great Hall. The Great Hall was 200 feet (61 meters) long and 100 feet (30 meters) wide. As the immigrants walked they passed doctors who gave them a "six-second physical." The doctors looked to make sure each person was breathing normally and acting normally. They looked for limping. Doctors also paid close attention to red or infected eyes. If they seemed healthy, immigrants moved on to a legal inspection. But if they did not pass the six-second physical, they were marked with chalk. This mark meant they needed a more thorough exam.

Going through these inspections could be scary. Immigrants sometimes were separated from their families or friends during the process. And until they made it through, everyone was worried that they could be sent back to where they came from. " … there were so many languages and so many people and everybody huddled together. And it was so full of fear," said Barbara Barondess, a Russian Jewish immigrant who was at Ellis Island in 1921.

◖◖ FACT ◗◗

The busiest years at Ellis Island were from 1900 to 1914. Between 5,000 and 10,000 people passed through every day.

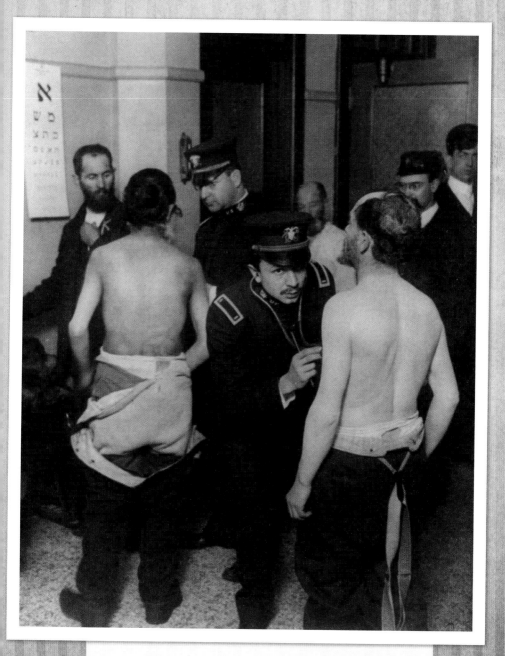

Uniformed doctors examined immigrants who had trouble breathing to learn if they suffered from heart or lung disease.

TREATING THE SICK

Those marked with chalk after the six-second physical went to the medical room. Doctors gave the immigrants a closer evaluation. If an immigrant was sick, he or she was taken to the hospital complex for treatment. Most of the patients at Ellis Island recovered with the help of the doctors and nurses. Once they were better, travelers were allowed into New York City.

Faye Lundky was one of the early immigrants to the island. She came in 1898 at the age of 5, but contracted measles on her way over from Russia. "They took me to the hospital ... and it was very frightening," she said. But she was treated by the doctors and nurses there and soon recovered. "When I got better [my father] took us to New York, and we lived on Cherry Street."

People with serious illnesses were given a bed and treated by doctors at the Ellis Island Immigrant Hospital.

Few immigrants were sent back to Europe because they had incurable diseases. Still, the process was scary for some. "The doctors and everybody else that were supposed to **interrogate** us were dressed in uniforms. … We were scared of uniforms. It took us back to the Russian uniforms that we were running away from," said Katherine Beychok, a Russian Jew who arrived in 1910.

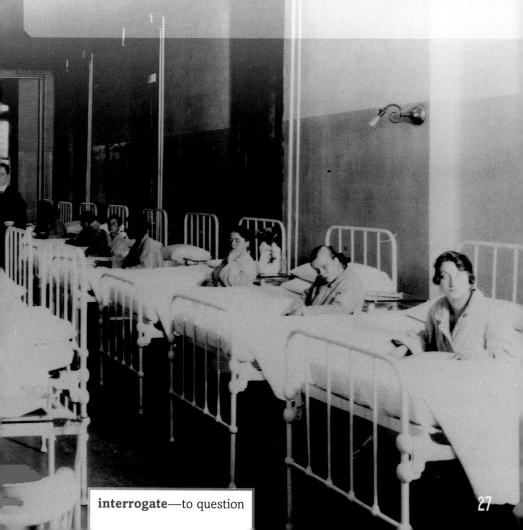

"The doctors and everybody else that were supposed to interrogate us were dressed in uniforms. … We were scared of uniforms."

interrogate—to question

LEGAL INSPECTIONS

Each steamship's crew gave Ellis Island officials the ship's manifest. The manifest included the information that had been collected about the immigrants before they left for America. For the legal inspection, immigrants waited in the Great Hall. An immigrant's name was called, and he or she would step forward to meet with an inspector. Inspectors asked immigrants questions from the forms to prove they were who they said they were. Russian immigrant William Chase was at Ellis Island in 1914. "I was very nervous because it was so noisy. I couldn't hear the names and I was afraid that I would miss my name and remain there forever."

Interpreters helped immigrants understand and answer the questions. But if an immigrant didn't answer a question correctly, he or she could be **detained** to sort out the problem. Those who were detained lived in a dormitory on the island while they waited for their case to be resolved. This process could take days or sometimes weeks.

Some immigrants who did not pass inspection were held in a separate area until they could be sent back to their country of origin.

detained—held like a prisoner

SENT BACK

———◦———

Immigrants who did not pass the legal inspection were sent back to their homelands. This could be very stressful. People had often spent all their money to get to America. So they had to return with nothing. In some cases one family member was sent back, while the rest of the family entered the United States. Sometimes these people never saw their families again. But being sent back was rare. Only about 2 percent of the people who came to Ellis Island failed to be admitted.

THE DORMITORIES

Most immigrants made it through Ellis Island in three to five hours. But one out of every five people stayed in dormitories while their cases were processed.

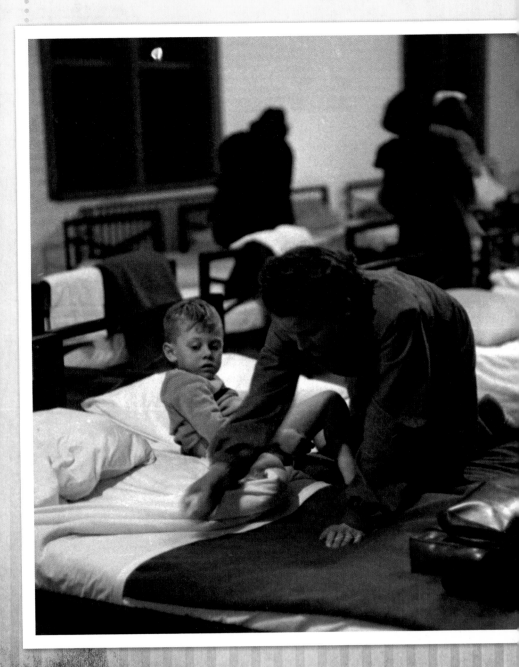

In the early days of Ellis Island, the dormitories were crowded and had bunks with no mattresses. But when Henry H. Curran became the Commissioner of Immigration in the 1920s, he decided to make upgrades. "I never saw a jail as bad as the dormitories on Ellis Island," he said. He replaced bunk bed cots with single beds that had mattresses. He also arranged for families to have private rooms.

Many immigrants were thankful, no matter how bad the conditions were. "I remember joy in Ellis Island," said Armenian immigrant Vartan Hartunian. "... in contrast to what I had gone through Ellis Island was ... but a heaven."

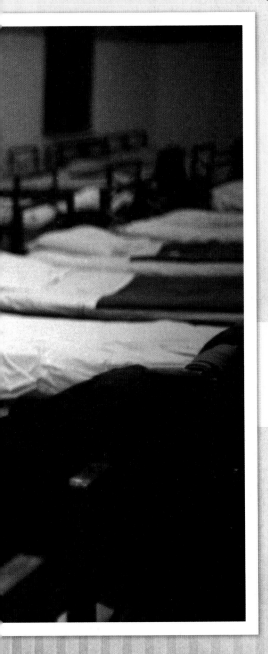

Beds were available for immigrants who stayed in the dormitories until they could leave.

" ... in contrast to what I had gone through Ellis Island was ... but a heaven."

THE DINING HALL

Many different foods were provided at no cost to the immigrants at Ellis Island. In the dining hall, they might be served beef stew and potatoes, bread and herring fish, or stewed prunes and baked beans. "[The dining room] was generally set very beautifully," said Vartan Hartunian. "… But when the people went in, it was like chaos … They would grab the butter. And if you didn't get there early enough, there was no butter left on the table."

Some immigrants were eating foods they had never seen before, such as bananas, ice cream, or oatmeal. "We got oatmeal for breakfast, and I didn't know what it was, with the brown sugar on it, you know. I couldn't get myself to eat it. So I put it on the windowsill, let the birds eat it," said Oreste Teglia, an Italian immigrant who arrived in 1916.

Many immigrants, such as these people in 1900, ate their first meal in the New World at Ellis Island's dining hall. The hall could fit up to 1,000 people.

MAKING IT OUT

Once immigrants passed all of the legal and medical inspections, they walked down a staircase at one end of the Great Hall. A post office and a railway ticketing office waited at the bottom of the stairs. Immigrants could also exchange their foreign money for American dollars. Social workers and other Ellis Island officers were there to help with any problems or questions.

Just outside the back doors of the main building was a place nicknamed the "kissing post." Families who had been separated during inspections frantically looked for each other there. People who already lived in New York also waited for their loved ones to come out. When they found each other, people kissed, hugged, and cried with joy.

Estelle Belford from Romania was 5 when she and her mother exited the main building at Ellis Island, "I remember my father puttin' his arms around my mother and the two of them … crying," she said. "And my father said to my mother, 'You're in America now and you have nothing to be afraid of.'"

Leaving Ellis Island was an experience filled with relief, uncertainty, and the wonder of possibility. "So, we all went down and got on the ferryboat. And the ferryboat ran to the Battery [in Manhattan]. And then, we just walked off, just like letting birds out of the cage," said Donald Roberts, a Welsh immigrant in 1925.

"And my father said to my mother, 'You're in America now and you have nothing to be afraid of.'"

CHAPTER FIVE

THE WORKERS ON ELLIS ISLAND

Roughly 500 employees worked at Ellis Island at any given time. Doctors, inspectors, interpreters, nurses, social workers, and other aid workers were always on hand to help arriving immigrants.

Doctors at Ellis Island became very good at spotting more than 50 diseases in just seconds. They also built a reputation for kindness. Josephine Calloway came to Ellis Island from Italy in 1922. She was so sick she had to stay in the hospital. "[The doctors] would come in and talk to me, and write to me in Latin, and then translate the word, they was trying to teach," said Calloway.

The nurses also tried to make the immigrants feel comfortable and safe. "....they talked to the children," said Elizabeth Martin from Hungary. "They stroked their hair. And they touched our cheeks and held our hands. ... some nurses would kiss the child on the cheek. They were really very nice."

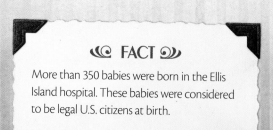

ೄಲ FACT ೨ಖ
More than 350 babies were born in the Ellis Island hospital. These babies were considered to be legal U.S. citizens at birth.

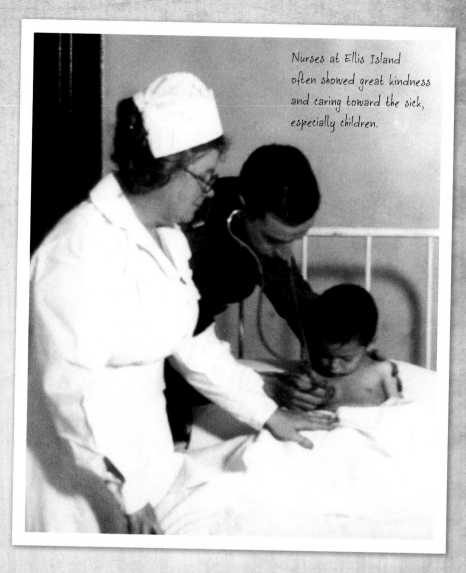

Nurses at Ellis Island often showed great kindness and caring toward the sick, especially children.

"They stroked their hair. And they touched our cheeks and held our hands. ... some nurses would kiss the child on the cheek. They were really very nice."

AID WORKERS

Aid workers gave counseling and provided immigrants with food, money, clothes, or a place to stay. Some were there for religious support.

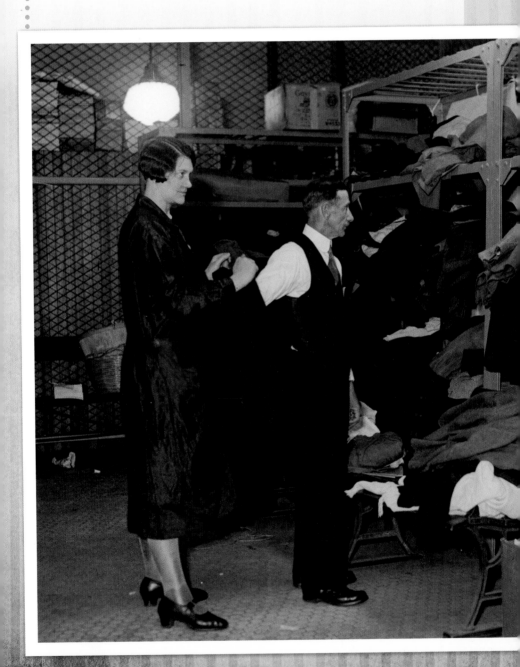

Ludmila Foxlee was a social worker at Ellis Island from 1920 through 1937. "They tell us that we help lighten the burden of detention with our daily visits," she said. "Above all this ... they want our friendliness ... almost all the people who need it get the friendly attention they crave."

These aid workers made sure immigrants had a place to go when they left the processing station. "Finally I got through and my brother who was supposed to claim me ... didn't show up so I'm waiting. They won't let me go on the ferryboat until I was claimed ..." remembered Manny Steen. "It's four o'clock. The island closed at four and the staff went home. Anyway, so they shipped me over to the depot on the other side of the island ... and I was held there ... They say, 'We close up here. Where's your ...?' I said, " I don't know." I had no phone or nothing. ... Anyway, they called up the HIAS, Hebrew Immigrant Aid Society, who would be responsible ... About fifteen minutes later this ... chap came in and ... he said 'Comm wit' [come with]."

Several religious organizations donated free clothing and other goods to help immigrants in need.

CORRUPTION

Not every worker on Ellis Island had good intentions. Over time some workers became involved with **corruption**. Sometimes they demanded bribes from immigrants or charged extra for railway tickets or food. Some cheated immigrants by lying about money exchange rates. But when President Theodore Roosevelt learned about these activities in 1901, he quickly acted to stop it. No longer would the mistreatment of immigrants be tolerated.

Early in 1902 Roosevelt appointed William Williams to be Commissioner of Immigration. Williams' job was to stop the corruption at Ellis Island. On June 23, 1902, Roosevelt wrote to Williams about improving the conditions. "… give me what your impressions are concerning the dishonesty and **malpractice**. … I am perfectly ready to fight if they insist upon having a fight over this matter."

corruption—dishonest behavior
malpractice—careless or wrong actions

Soon workers were awarded for good behavior and punished for illegal behavior or dishonesty. Services for the immigrants were improved too. Signs that said "Kindness and Consideration" were posted to remind workers of the respect they were to show immigrants.

Inspectors questioned immigrants to make sure they were who they claimed to be. But some inspectors became corrupt. They demanded that immigrants pay money before letting them enter New York.

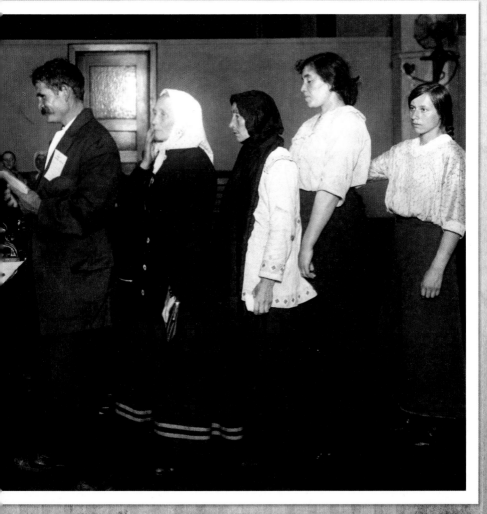

CHAPTER SIX

THE WAVE OF IMMIGRATION ENDS

During World War I (1914–1918) most immigration to America came to a halt. After the war Congress passed laws limiting the number of immigrants who were allowed to come into the country. Then the Great Depression that began in 1929 destroyed most of the job opportunities that once existed. Immigration slowed to a trickle.

But a few immigrants still came, such as those who left Europe after World War II (1939–1945). And for them, Ellis Island was still the beacon of hope and freedom it had been for its very first visitors. "In America I didn't have to be afraid," said Marcia Press. "America gave me and my parents the opportunity to live in a place where you could be whatever you wanted to be. You could have dreams. And they might actually come true."

Between 1925 and 1954, only about 2.5 million immigrants were processed at Ellis Island. In 1954 the U.S. government ended immigration operations and shut down Ellis Island.

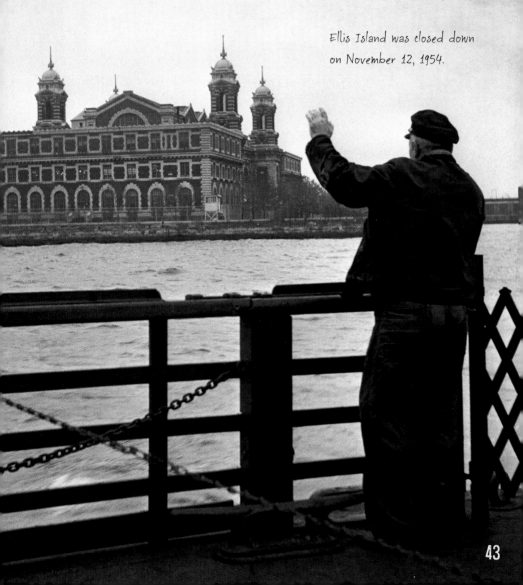

"America gave me and my parents the opportunity to live in a place where you could be whatever you wanted to be. You could have dreams. And they might actually come true."

Ellis Island was closed down on November 12, 1954.

ELLIS ISLAND TODAY

In 1965 Ellis Island was added to the Statue of Liberty National Monument. It is now open to the public for visits. In the Ellis Island Museum, people can look through the millions of immigrant arrival records.

Ellis Island remains the most powerful reminder of America's immigrant history. From a mud patch it became a small city that welcomed courageous immigrants. The people who came through Ellis Island went on to build new lives. And they also helped turn the United States into the diverse nation it is today.

Today visitors to Ellis Island can walk through the Great Hall and see some of the luggage that immigrants carried with them from their home countries.

PRIMARY SOURCES

Primary sources appear on the following pages:

Pages 6, 10, 15, 20, 24, 27, 28, 31, 32, 35, 36, 39, from *Ellis Island: An Illustrated History of the Immigrant Experience* by Ivan Chermayeff, Fred Wasserman, and Mary J. Shapiro. (New York: Maxwell Macmillan International, 1991.)

Page 9, from Congressional Serial Set. U.S. Government Printing Office, 1891 - United States.

Page 9, from "New Immigration Depot: The Buildings on Ellis Island," the New York Daily Tribune, December 27, 1891.

Page 12, from "Federal Buildings in Ruins: Flames Sweep Over Ellis Island Doing Great Damage," the San Francisco Call, June 15, 1897.

Pages 16, 19, 21, 42, Marcia Press, interview by Danny Kravitz, September 3, 2014.

Pages 18, 23, 39, Emanuel "Manny" Steen, interview by Paul E. Sigrist, Jr., March 22, 1991, Ellis Island Oral History Collection.

Page 19, Willian Greiner, interview by Paul E. Sigrist, Jr., March 3, 1991, Ellis Island Oral History Collection.

Page 21, Lawrence Meinwald, interview by Paul E. Sigrist, Jr., May 29, 1991, Ellis Island Oral History Collection.

Page 26, from *Toward a Better Life: America's New Immigrants in Their Own Words: From Ellis Island to the Present* by Peter Morton Coan. (Amherst, N.Y.: Prometheus Books, 2011.)

Page 35, Estelle Belford, interview by Paul E. Sigrist, Jr., May 14, 1991, Ellis Island Oral History Collection.

Page 40, from letter from Theodore Roosevelt to William Williams. June 23, 1902. Online by the Theodore Roosevelt Center at Dickinson State University. http://www.theodorerooseveltcenter.org/Research/Digital-Library/Record.aspx?libID=o182637

GLOSSARY

amenities (uh-MEN-uh-teez)—items other than the very basic necessities

corruption (kuh-RUP-shuhn)—dishonest behavior

detained (dee-TAIND)—held like a prisoner

interpreter (in-TUR-prit-uhr)—a person who can tell others what is said in another language

interrogate (in-TER-uh-gate)—to question

malpractice (mal-PRAK-tus)—careless or wrong actions

manifest (MAN-uh-fest)—a list of passengers on a ship

persecution (pur-suh-CUE-shuhn)—cruel or unfair treatment, often because of race or religious beliefs

processed (PRAH-sessd)—put through a series of tasks

vaccination (vak-suh-NAY-shuhn)—a shot of medicine that protects from a disease

READ MORE

Bliss, John. *Nineteenth Century Migration to America.* Children's True Stories: Migration. Chicago: Raintree, 2012.

Burgan, Michael. *Ellis Island: An Interactive History Adventure.* You Choose: History. North Mankato, Minn.: Capstone Press, 2013.

McDaniel, Melissa. *Ellis Island.* Cornerstones of Freedom. New York: Children's Press, 2011.

CRITICAL THINKING
USING THE COMMON CORE

1. Compare Henry Curran's quotation on page 31 with the quotation from Vartan Hartunian on the same page. Why did their perspectives about the conditions of the Ellis Island dormitories differ? *(Integration of Knowledge and Ideas)*

2. Why was the Statue of Liberty such an important sight for incoming immigrants? Use other resources to support your answer. *(Integration of Knowledge and Ideas)*

INTERNET SITES

FactHound offers a safe, fun way to find Internet sites related to this book. All of the sites on FactHound have been researched by our staff.

Here's all you do:
Visit *www.facthound.com*
Type in this code: 9781491441275

INDEX